Luisa Rose
Fröhliche Reigenspiele
Ausmalbuch für Erwachsene

Bibliografische Information der Deutschen Nationalbibliothek:
Die Deutsche Nationalbibliothek verzeichnet diese Publikation in der
Deutschen Nationalbibliografie; detaillierte bibliografische
Daten sind im Internet über http://dnb.dnb.de abrufbar.

© 2016 Luisa Rose; 1. Auflage
Covergrafik, Texte & Illustrationen © 2016 Luisa Rose

Herstellung und Verlag: BoD – Books on Demand, Norderstedt

ISBN: 9783743104112

Build it up with iron bars,
 Iron bars, iron bars,
Build it up with iron bars
 My fair lady.

Build it up with pins & needles,
 Pins & needles, pins & needles.
Build it up with pins & needles
 My fair lady.

Build it up with penny loaves,
 Penny loaves, penny loaves,
Build it up with penny loaves
 My fair lady.

Iron bars will rust away,
 Rust away, rust away
Iron bars will rust away
 My fair lady.

Pins & needles rust & bend,
 Rust & bend, rust & bend,
Pins & needles rust & bend
 My fair lady.

Penny loaves will tumble down,
 Tumble down, tumble down,
Penny loaves will tumble down
 My fair lady.

LONDON BRIDGE — Continued

Build it up with gold & silver
  Gold & silver, gold & silver,
Build it up with gold & silver
  My fair lady.

Gold & silver I have not got
  Have not got, have not got,
Gold & silver I have not got
  My fair lady.

Here's a prisoner I have got
  I have got, I have got,
Here's a prisoner I have got
  My fair lady.

What's the prisoner done to you,
  Done to you, done to you,
What's the prisoner done to you
  My fair lady.

LONDON BRIDGE CONCLUDED

Stole my watch & broke my chain,
  Broke my chain, broke my chain,
Stole my watch & broke my chain
    My fair lady.

One hundred pounds will set him free,
  Set him free, set him free,
One hundred pounds will set him free
    My fair lady.

Then off to prison you must go,
  You must go, you must go,
Then off to prison you must go
    My fair lady.

What will you take to set him free
  Set him free, set him free,
What will you take to set him free
    My fair lady.

One hundred pounds we have not got,
  Have not got, have not got,
One hundred pounds we have not got
    My fair lady.

Oh! sleep sleep daughter do not wake
Here are three sailors whom we can't take
You cannot have a lodging here, here, here
You cannot have a lodging here.

Here come three soldiers three by three
To court your daughter a fair lady
Can we have a lodging here, here, here
Can we have a lodging here.

Oh' sleep sleep daughter do not wake
Here are three soldiers whom we can't take.
You cannot have a lodging here, here, here
You cannot have a lodging here.

HERE·COME·THREE·SAILORS·
Continued

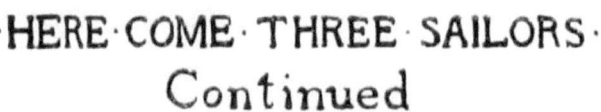

Here come three Kings three by three
To court your daughter a fair lady
Can we have a lodging here, here, here
Can we have a lodging here.

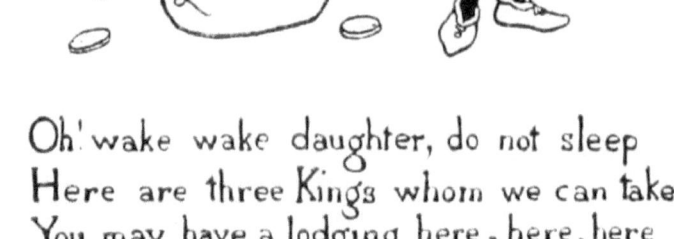

Oh! wake wake daughter, do not sleep
Here are three Kings whom we can take
You may have a lodging here, here, here
You may have a lodging here.

Here's my daughter safe and sound
And in her pocket one hundred pound
And on her finger a gay gold ring
I am sure she is fit to walk with a King.

LOOBY LOO CONTINUED

Here we dance looby loo
Here we dance looby light
Here we dance looby loo
All on a Saturday night

All your left hands in
All your left hands out little
Shake your left hands a little a
And turn yourselves about.

Here we dance looby loo
Here we dance looby light
Here we dance looby loo
All on a Saturday night.

All your right feet in
All your right feet out little
Shake your right feet a little, a
And turn yourselves about.

Here we dance looby loo
Here we dance looby light
Here we dance looby loo
All on a Saturday night.

All your left feet in
All your left feet out   little
Shake all your left feet a little a
And turn yourselves about.

LOOBY LOO CONCLUDED

Here we dance looby, loo
Here we dance looby light
Here we dance looby, loo
All on a Saturday night.

All your noddles in
All your noddles out   La little
Shake all your noddles a little
And turn yourselves about.

Here we dance looby, loo
Here we dance looby, light
Here we dance looby, loo
All on a Saturday night.

Put all yourselves in
Put all yourselves out   little
Shake all yourselves a little a
And turn yourselves about.

ROUND·AND·ROUND·THE·VILLAGE

In and out the windows, In and out the windows,
In and out the windows, As we have done before.

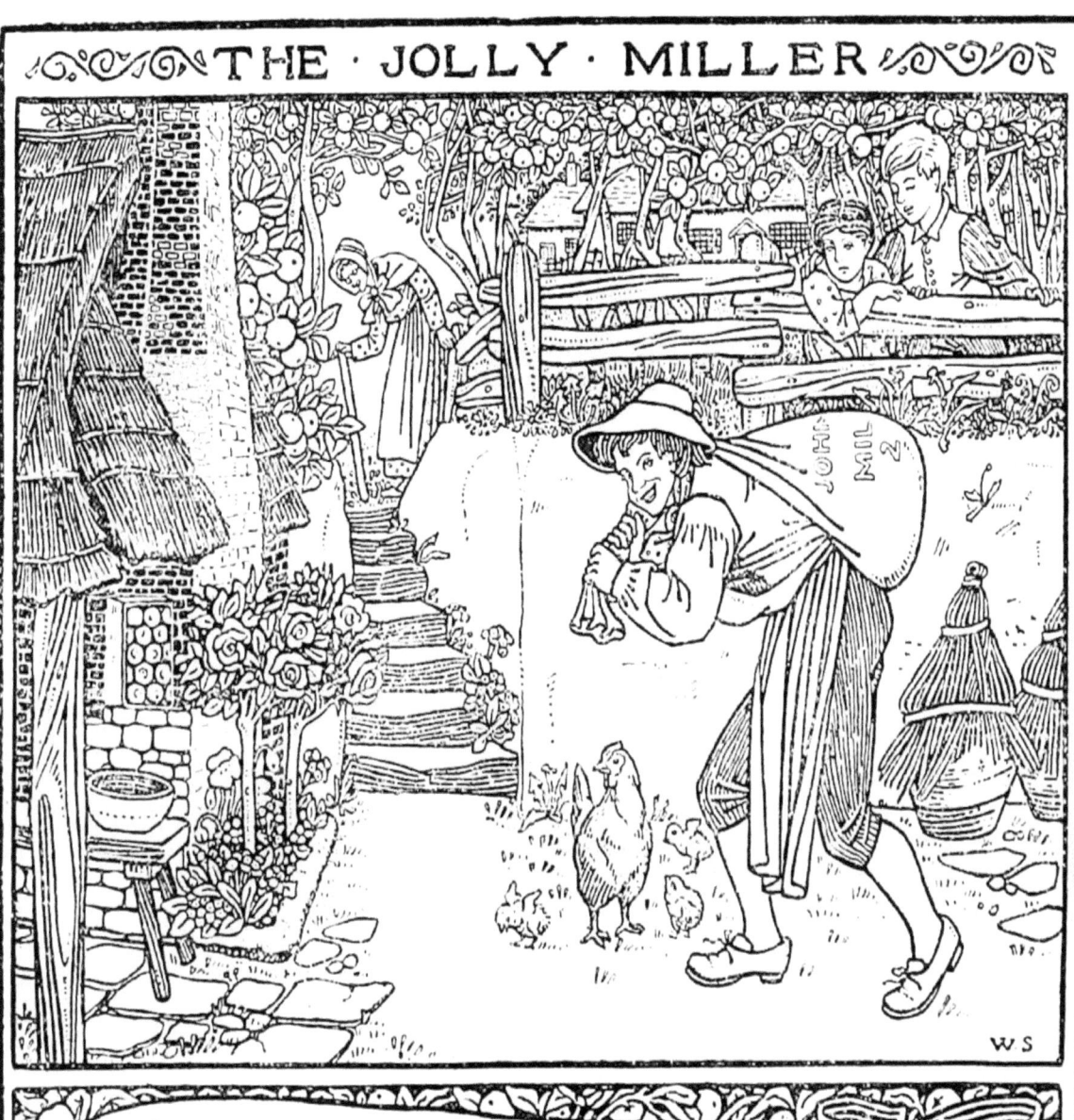

THE · JOLLY · MILLER

There was a jolly miller and he lived by himself.

OATS AND BEANS AND BARLEY GROW

First the farmer sows his seed,
Then he stands and takes his ease,
Stamps his foot and claps his hands
And turns him round to view the land.

Weitere Ausmalbücher von Luisa Rose:

Titel	ISBN
Alice im Wunderland	9783741297502
Blumen und Märchen	9783743102002
Der Struwwelpeter	9783743102699
Die Struwwelliese	9783743102811
Don Quixote	9783743104037
Drei kleine Schweine	9783743104099
Eine Blumenhochzeit	9783743104105
Fröhliche Reigenspiele	9783743104112
Lustige Tanzspiele	9783743104273
Reise ins antike Griechenland	9783743112568
Flucht ins antike Griechenland	9783743112599
Pariser Leben im 19.Jahrhundert	9783743112704
Die Sommerkönigin	9783743112742
Der Schneider und die Krähe	9783743112827
Die Wikinger	9783743113275
Hänsel und Gretel	9783743114265
Max und Moritz	9783743103214
Schnurrdirburr	9783743112834
Mode des 18. und 19. Jahrhunderts	9783743112971
Kostümbilder des 18. und 19. Jahrhunderts	9783743114401
Abenteuer im Bienenland	9783743117051
Griechische Helden der Antike	9783743117709
Märchen alter Zeit	9783743116559

Notizbücher von Luisa Rose:

Titel	ISBN
Drachentöter (Notizbuch)	9783743113077
Natures Wonders (Notizbuch)	9783743113817
Gedankenspiel Notizen (Notizbuch)	9783743113886
Smaragd Notizen (Notizbuch)	9783743114296
Jagd Notizen (Notizbuch)	9783743114302
Tradition (Notizbuch)	9783743114319
Antik Notizbuch (Notizbuch)	9783743114326
Veni Vidi Vici (Notizbuch)	9783743114340
Black List (Notizbuch)	9783743114371
Mystic Notes (Notizbuch)	9783743114388
Magic Notes (Notizbuch)	9783743114418
Fantasien (Notizbuch)	9783743114463
Creative Notes (Notizbuch)	9783743114487
Persönliche Notizen (Notizbuch)	9783743114494
Peter Pan (Notizbuch)	9783743114531
Rose (Notizbuch)	9783743114548
Quality Street (Notizbuch)	9783743114555
Rubin Notizen (Notizbuch)	9783743114647
Schmetterlinge (Notizbuch)	9783743114661
Ali Baba (Notizbuch)	9783743114678
The portrait of a Lady (Notizbuch)	9783743114692
Shakespeare (Notizbuch)	9783743114722
Brainstorming (Notizbuch)	9783743114739
Merlin (Notizbuch)	9783743114746
Rügen (Notizbuch)	9783743114784

Möchtest du über neue Bücher von Luisa Rose per email Informiert werden? Dann schicke eine Email mit ‚Newsletter' im Betreff an Luisa.Rose@t-online.de